Contents

Impact!	2
Flood and fire forum	4
Get ready! Get set! Survive!	7
High and dry	9
Black Saturday fire disaster	13
Strands in action	16

Impact!

"The weather may break our hearts but it will not break our will."

Anna Bligh, Queensland Premier (2007–2012) in response to the 2011 floods

Floods and bushfires are common in many places in Australia. Both have an enormous impact on the environment and on communities, often in devastating ways. They can kill and injure people and animals. They can destroy forests, homes, farms, roads, schools, shops and even whole towns.

Some bushfires and floods can have beneficial impacts, such as stimulating animals to breed and plants to **germinate**.

People who live in flood- and bushfire-prone areas need to be prepared, so they can remain safe when these disasters occur.

Floods and bushfires are a part of nature and can never be stopped. Governments and communities are continually improving the way they respond to these disasters, in an attempt to lessen their destructive impact.

Did you know?

In 1990, the small town of Nyngan, in New South Wales was **inundated** with floodwater, even after the townspeople laid 260 000 sandbags. Nearly every resident had to be airlifted to safety. Interestingly, the Aboriginal meaning of the word Nyngan is 'long pond of water', or flood!

LET'S FIND OUT

- How do floods and bushfires impact the environment?
- How do floods and bushfires impact communities?
- How do communities in flood and bushfire areas prepare for these disasters?
- What actions and processes are put in place to respond when floods or bushfires strike?
- What actions can minimise the impact of floods and fires on communities?

germinate begin to grow
inundated totally covered in water

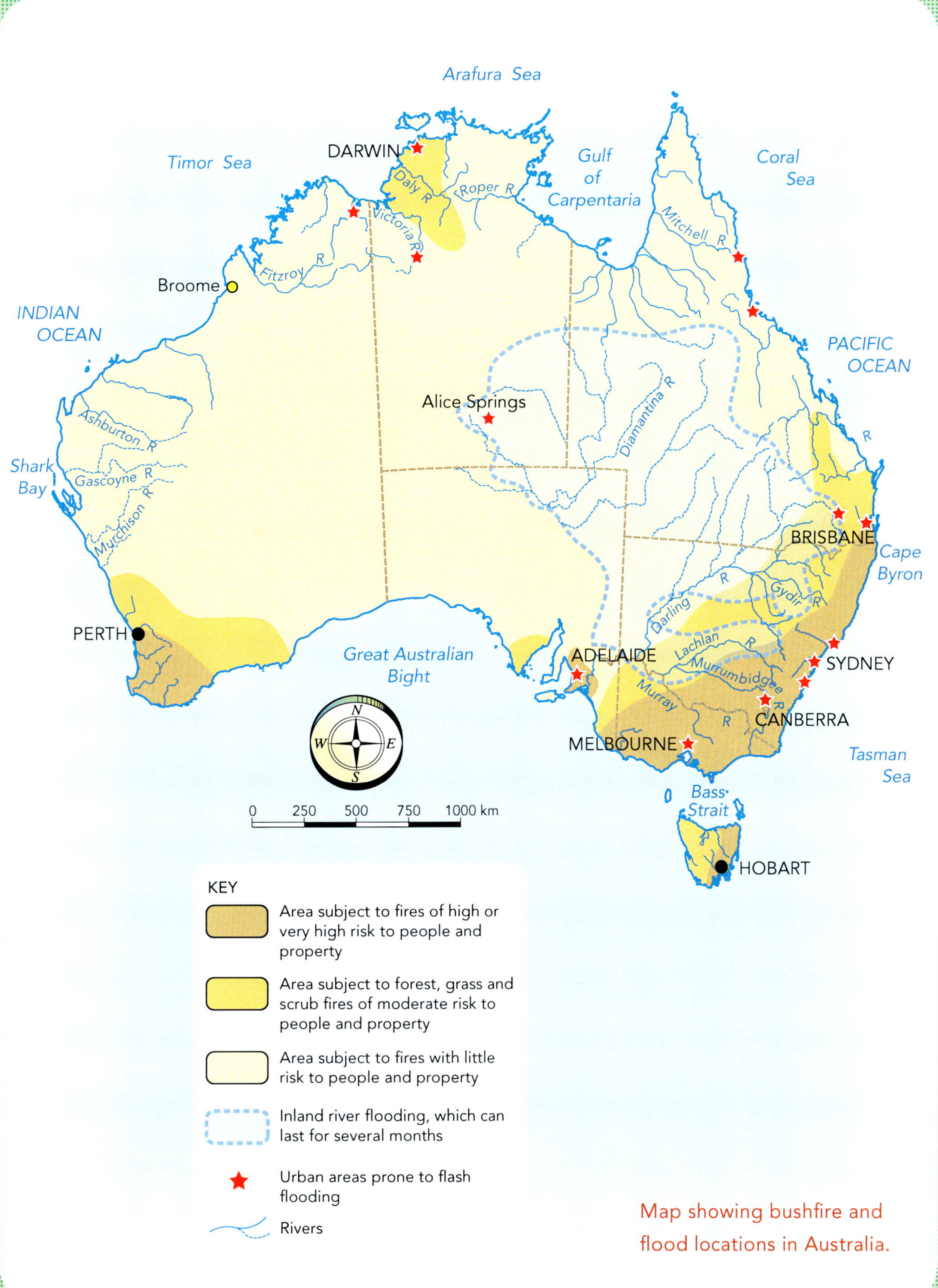

Map showing bushfire and flood locations in Australia.

Flood and fire forum

Carmen Green: Hello and welcome to today's forum – floods and fires in Australia. Our guests are Professor Robert Kim, an expert on the history of bushfires and floods in Australia, and Doctor Sue Grant, from the Department of the Environment. I am your host, Carmen Green.

Professor Kim, how do fires and floods impact the environment?

Professor Kim: Well, the most obvious impact is the enormous loss of plants and animals. For example, the 2009 Black Saturday bushfires all but destroyed the only known habitat of the Leadbeater's possum, which is now close to extinction. These fires increased the amount of **carbon dioxide** (CO_2) in the air and polluted **water catchments** with ash.

Australian Leadbeater's possum

Doctor Grant: Fires and floods have some positive impacts. Floods can end long droughts, top up water supplies and **dilute** salt in the soil. After floods, waterbirds have more food and therefore breed more. Areas regenerate after bushfires – fire cracks open seeds and seed-pods in some species, allowing plants to germinate. Some plants grow better after fire, as they receive more sun and have less competition.

A flood inundating houses in Brisbane

Carmen Green: And how do floods and fires impact communities?

carbon dioxide gas made by burning carbon
water catchments large stores of water saved for human use
dilute to thin out

Doctor Grant: The most devastating impact is the loss of life and the destruction of towns and communities. Fires and floods damage properties, businesses, livestock, crops and the **infrastructure** of towns and cities. This is extremely costly. Floods alone cost Australia an average of 377 million dollars a year! And the emotional cost on people is impossible to calculate.

The practice of fire-stick burning reduces fuel.

Carmen Green: So, what is the answer? How do we live with these deadly natural events?

Professor Kim: Whether people should live in flood- and fire-**prone** areas is something that is constantly debated. For example, should people build homes on flood plains where there is regular flooding? The statistics would indicate not, but there's more to consider than just numbers.

Doctor Grant: It comes down to reducing the impact these disasters have. For example, in bushfire areas, homes should use the safest materials and designs.

Carmen Green: What about reducing branches and undergrowth that fuel bushfires?

Professor Kim: Reducing fuel decreases the chances of bushfires becoming enormous and out of control. We can learn from Aboriginal and Torres Strait Islander people in this area who, for tens of thousands of years, have burnt large areas of bush, using a method called fire-stick burning. This thinned out trees and undergrowth, which avoided the large **catastrophic** fires that we see today.

Carmen Green: Professor Kim and Doctor Grant, thank you for your time. You've given us much to consider! ”

infrastructure structures in a town or city such as bridges, roads and power stations
prone very likely to experience something
catastrophic causing sudden, enormous damage and suffering

Breakaway tasks

Remembering

1 Take turns with a partner, telling each other a flood or fire fact. How many facts can you recall?

2 What is one way that Aboriginal and Torres Strait Islander people managed the land? How did this lessen the severe impact of bushfires?

Understanding

3 In a group of three, act out the forum.

4 Create a ten-question multiple-choice quiz about floods and fires. Swap quizzes with a classmate and complete each other's quizzes.

5 Create a visual representation of how floods or bushfires can have a positive impact on the environment.

Applying

6 Continue the interview:
- Write two more questions for Doctor Grant and two more questions for Professor Kim.
- Research to find the answers to your questions.
- Write the answers in the voices of Doctor Grant and Professor Kim.

Analysing

7 On a data chart, identify and record the positive and negative impacts that bushfires and floods have on the environment.

	Floods	Bushfires
Positive impacts		
Negative impacts		

8 Use a Similar and different chart to compare floods and bushfires.

Evaluating

9 Evaluate whether you think people should live in flood- or bushfire-prone areas. Write reasons for your opinion.

Creating

10 Plan and present a 2–5 minute oral presentation on the traditional Aboriginal and Torres Strait Islander land management practice of fire-stick burning. Use research skills to find information to include in your presentation.

GET READY! GET SET! SURVIVE!

Bushfires kill! Are YOU prepared?

GET READY!

Embers can be blown over 10 kilometres ahead of the main fire.

Prepare your home!

- Clean out gutters.
- Clear away thick vegetation.
- Remove dry grass and twigs from your lawn.
- Cut back tree branches close to your home.
- Remove large shrubs close to windows.
- Remove **flammable** items, such as paint, petrol, chemicals and gas bottles.

Get set!

You MUST be organised! A fire can travel over 100 kilometres in an hour.

Get organised!

- Prepare a bushfire emergency plan.
- Discuss your plan with the whole family – everyone must know what to do in an emergency.
- Prepare an emergency supply kit (portable battery-operated radio, torch, spare batteries, bottled water, first aid kit, candles with waterproof matches, woollen blankets, medications, tinned food).

- Place valuables and precious items in a box (include important documents, photos, certificates and so on) in case you need to **evacuate**.

Survive!

Survival is all that matters! Bushfires are dangerous.

When a bushfire emergency strikes:

- stay informed – listen to the radio, access websites, monitor your mobile phone for emergency alerts
- implement your safety plan.

---

embers small pieces of burning material blown from the main fire
flammable something that catches fire and burns easily
evacuate to leave a place if danger is on the way

Breakaway tasks

Remembering

1 From memory, list five things you should do to prepare for bushfires.

2 Draw and label a sketch showing a house and yard that is well prepared for bushfires.

Understanding

3 With a partner, discuss how people might find out if there is a bushfire emergency in their area.

4 In small groups, discuss the purpose of the poster. Why would a poster like this be created?

Applying

5 Use research skills to find examples of real fire safety advertisements. Use a table to describe how these advertisements are similar and different to the one on page 7.

6 Write a letter to take home to your family discussing the importance of having a fire safety plan.

Analysing

7 On a T-chart, list five things that the poster encourages you to do to prepare for bushfires and list the reasons why these things should be done.

8 How are people made aware of disasters that are predicted for their area? Investigate the various emergency alert systems used and report back to the class.

Evaluating

9 Rate the effectiveness of the poster out of 10. What was the intended message? How well was this message delivered? What features of the poster convinced you to be fire ready?

Creating

10 Investigate fire safety plans, such as plans for your school or for your home. Use ideas from these to develop a fire safety plan for your home. Include evacuation and meeting points.

High and dry

"Look at the creek!" exclaimed Ruby, from her **vantage point** on top of the old fire-viewing tower.

"The water's rising rapidly," Patrick observed. "And it's still pelting down!"

"We'd better head home and warn Mum and Dad," Ruby concluded.

Ruby and Patrick scrambled down the steps of the rickety old tower, jumped on their bikes and pedalled furiously home.

Half an hour later, they reached the old-style farmhouse, perched high on top of a hill in the middle of their cattle property.

"Mum, Dad!" bellowed Patrick. "The creek has almost **ruptured** its banks!"

"I warned you not to approach the creek in foul weather like this," Mum scolded.

"We didn't," objected Ruby. "We saw it from the tower – "

"What?" Dad interrupted. "That tower's a death trap! You must promise to never climb it again!"

Ruby and Patrick nodded as their parents exchanged worried glances.

Their father addressed them like troops before a battle. "I've checked the weather forecast and this could be the most severe flood we've ever experienced. We must herd the cattle to higher ground … and quickly. Ruby, you come with me in the ute."

Mum turned to Patrick, "I need your help at the school, where everyone is sandbagging. Hopefully we can prevent the school being damaged like it was in the 2005 flood."

vantage point a place from which a person can view something
ruptured burst

The rain hammered down relentlessly, making visibility difficult, even with the windscreen wipers on full speed.

"We must move the cattle out of this rising water," Dad insisted. "Otherwise, they'll get **foot rot**, be stranded without any feed, or worse still, they could be swept away and drown."

It was strenuous work in the driving rain, but Ruby and her dad managed to herd all of the frightened cattle into the highest paddock on the farm.

"They'll be secure here," said Dad, relieved, as he padlocked the gate. "Great job. Now, let's go!"

Rain fell in sheets and flooded the rough track that led back to the house. Dad gripped the steering wheel so tightly his knuckles turned white, and fixed his gaze on the track ahead. The track itself was slick and moving, like a snake, slithering towards their home. It was treacherous.

Suddenly, out of the blue, the ute lost **traction** and the vehicle slid out of control.

Ruby screamed.

BANG!

They slammed into the trunk of a massive eucalypt. The front of the ute crumpled like a scrap of paper.

foot rot a serious infection that affects the feet of cattle

traction grip between two surfaces such as a car tyre and the road

Narrative

"Dad," sobbed Ruby, "there's blood on your head!"

"I'm fine," he winced. "It's just a cut, but … I think my arm could be broken."

"I'll call Mum," said Ruby, gulping back hot tears.

But the call wouldn't connect.

"There's probably no reception in this **gully**," explained Dad, as he cradled his arm to his chest and studied the damaged ute.

"This ute's not going anywhere," he sighed. "We'll have to walk."

So they cautiously began the long trek home, step by careful step as the rain relentlessly pounded into them. When they reached the creek, what Ruby saw made her heart race like a frightened rabbit.

"The bridge!" Ruby choked.

The bridge that once crossed a lazy creek was now totally **submerged** under fast-gushing water that sped along like a bullet train.

Dad and Ruby exchanged desperate looks; this was their only way home. How would they escape the rapidly rising water?

"I know," announced Dad in a firm, decisive voice. "We'll climb the old fire tower … and wait."

"But Dad?" ventured Ruby. "You said it's dangerous."

"It's our only option," he asserted.

It kept raining cats and dogs as they trekked through soggy ground until they reached the tower.

"Up you go," said Dad. "I'll be right behind you."

The tower groaned like a wounded animal as Ruby and her dad clambered to the top. Once there, they huddled together, exhausted but relieved.

"Here," said Dad, putting on a brave face. "Let's give the phone another try."

This time it worked!

Ruby explained everything to her shocked mother, who promised to send help.

Hours later, as they sat imprisoned in their tower, a strange whirr made Ruby look into the bleak, grey sky. And, as the sound drew closer, Ruby saw the **beacon** of a rescue helicopter. It was coming for them! They were going to be okay.

gully a small valley
submerged covered by water
beacon signal

Breakaway tasks

Remembering

1 Why were Ruby and her Dad out in the rain? Why couldn't they drive back to the house?

2 Sketch one of the scenes in the story.

3 Retell the main events in the story to a partner.

Understanding

4 In a table, record the advantages and disadvantages of the decision Ruby's dad made to climb the tower and wait for help. What would you have done in this situation? Why?

5 Create a true or false quiz about this story. Swap your quiz with a classmate and complete each other's quizzes.

Applying

6 Use research skills to find out about different types of floods (flash-floods, sea water floods and slow-moving floods). Create a slide show to present this information to the class.

7 With a partner or in a small group, act out a scene or the whole story, adding dialogue.

Analysing

8 Report on the story in terms of setting, characters, problem and resolution.

Evaluating

9 Plot the highs and lows of the story using a line graph. On the horizontal axis, write the main events from the story. On the vertical axis, record the numbers from one to ten. Place a dot for each event next to a number in terms of how you rate the drama or excitement of that event (10 being extremely exciting and 0 being boring). Use a ruler to join the dots.

Creating

10 Plan and write a newspaper article about Ruby and her father's rescue. Include information about the event (what happened and how it was resolved) and quotes from Ruby and her dad. Include a catchy headline and images to illustrate your article.

Black Saturday fire disaster

In 2009, massive bushfires raced through Victoria causing widespread destruction. Below is a transcript of a news bulletin about these fires from the ABC program, *Behind the News*.

Fire – it's one of our most useful tools and a part of daily life. But out of control, it can instantly become one of the deadliest forces on the planet.

The weekend from hell started with dire warnings from fire-fighters and the weather bureau. They were expecting high winds, dry air and record temperatures. All in all, they feared that if any fires started, they would be impossible to fight. And they were.

Thirty-one fires ripped through the state, destroying whole towns in minutes. [Residents in their path] say they were given little or no warning of how bad it would be.

Scientists say it was like 500 atomic bombs worth of heat being released on these small communities ...

The devastating damage caused by the Black Saturday fires

transcript copy
dire extremely serious

Town after town, area after area were destroyed. More than 450000 **hectares** were burnt, including around 2000 houses. But worse than that was the number of lives lost. One hundred and eighty-nine people have been confirmed dead and maybe a million animals also lost their lives. It was easily Australia's worst natural disaster in history.

Nathan Bazley, reporter: But why was it so deadly? Well to answer that, we need to know how a bushfire can go from a tiny spark to a massive **inferno**.

There are a few factors [that] can make a small fire turn into something like Saturday's destructive blaze. The weather is one. On the day of the fires, there was 47-degree heat in Victoria, along with very dry, but very powerful winds. The heat made fuel – like wood and leaves – burn much easier.

Wind pushed flames through the bush at more than 120 kilometres an hour and blew burning embers up to 15 kilometres from the fire itself. This created all new fire fronts with frightening speed. They were the worst conditions ever recorded.

Another factor that made this fire so devastating is the areas that it hit. Much of the parts of Victoria that were burnt are hilly and covered in eucalyptus trees [...] Fires travel much faster uphill and eucalypts are highly flammable because of the oil in their leaves [...]

Many [people injured in the fires] will take years to get back to full health. How long it will take their communities to recover is far less certain.

Plant regrowth after a bushfire

hectares unit of measurement that measures area of land
inferno huge, out-of-control fire

Breakaway tasks

Remembering

1 List statistics mentioned in the news transcript.

2 List alternative words used for 'fire' in the news transcript.

Understanding

3 With a partner, take turns to retell what you have learnt about the Black Saturday fires.

4 Imagine you are the weather forecaster on the day of the Black Saturday fires. Announce the weather conditions on that hot and windy day.

5 With a partner, discuss why people feared that if any fires started on this day, "they would be impossible to fight"?

Applying

6 Create a sketch showing the regeneration of plants after a bushfire.

7 What else would you like to know about the Black Saturday fires? Write three questions and use research skills to find the answers.

Analysing

8 Analyse the reasons why the Black Saturday fires were so destructive. Use the Web plus writing pro forma to record your ideas. Begin by writing 'Black Saturday fires' in the centre circle. In the other four circles, give reasons explaining why the fires were so ferocious. Branching out from these, note the effect of each of the reasons you recorded.

Evaluating

9 The news transcript calls these fires "easily Australia's worst natural disaster in history". Do you agree with this evaluation? Justify your answer.

Creating

10 Create a plan to minimise the impact of a bushfire. Think about:

- ways to prevent a fire starting
- ways to prepare for a bushfire
- ways to warn people when horrific weather is on the way
- ways to inform people about evacuating if a fire starts.

Present your plan orally to the class or create a poster.

Strands in action

Core tasks

1 Design and create an animation about being prepared for bushfires or floods.
  - Include what they are, why they are dangerous and how to remain safe during the event.
  - Invent a cartoon character to promote either bushfire or flood safety and use the character in your animation.

2 Design, plan and present a flood and bushfire quiz show.
  - Research flood and fire facts.
  - Write at least 15 quiz questions and answers. These could be any format (for example, question and answer, multiple-choice, 'What am I?' questions).
  - Plan your quiz show including the format, host, the number of contestants, prizes and so on.
  - Organise classmates to be involved.
  - Present your quiz show to the class (alternatively, you could film your show).

Extra tasks

1 Complete a concept map about floods or bushfires.

2 Write a cinquain poem about bushfires or floods. Present your poem in an interesting way.

3 Think about how bushfires and floods impact the environment. In what ways is their impact the same? How is their impact different? Use a Venn diagram to record your ideas. Share your diagram with three other students and combine your ideas to create a large, group Venn diagram.

4 Research volunteer firefighters – how to become one, what training is required, what their role is on a bushfire day. Write a report on your findings. Include images.

A **clause** expresses meaning. A simple sentence contains one clause, e.g. *The cat is on the mat.* A complex sentence has an independent clause (the main message) and a dependent clause (extra information about that message), e.g. *The cat is on the mat outside the back door.* When writing narratives, experiment with using a mix of complex and simple sentences to build drama.